–Fast Tracks

–Drag Racing

A.T. McKenna

visit us at
www.abdopub.com

Published by Abdo & Daughters, 4940 Viking Drive, Suite 622, Edina, Minnesota 55435.
Copyright © 1998 by Abdo Consulting Group, Inc., Pentagon Tower, P.O. Box 36036, Minneapolis, Minnesota 55435 USA. International copyrights reserved in all countries. No part of this book may be reproduced in any form without written permission from the publisher.

Printed in the United States.

Cover and Interior Photo credits: Allsport USA, Duomo, SportsChrome

Edited by Paul Joseph

Library of Congress Cataloging-in-Publication Data

Mckenna, A. T.
    Drag racing / A. T. McKenna.
       p. cm. -- (Fast tracks)
  Includes index.
  Summary: An overview of drag racing with descriptions of the drag strip, Christmas tree lights, driver gear, racing fuel, time trials, and race day. Includes a glossary of terms.
   ISBN 1-56239-836-9
  1. Drag racing--Juvenile literature.   [1. Drag racing.]
  I. Title II. Series: McKenna, A. T. Fast tracks
  GV1029.3.M39 1998
  796.72--dc21   97-31055
                                                     CIP
                                                     AC

−Contents

–Drag Racing

At speeds of around 300 miles per hour (483 kilometers per hour), drag racing is the fastest form of auto racing in the United States. The sport started out as a contest of speed. Two cars were placed side-by-side. The cars raced down a street or country road in a straight line (called a strip). The first car to reach the finish line was the winner.

This wasn't really an accurate test though, since the two cars competing could have many differences. One car could be larger in size than the other or the engine in one car could be more powerful than the other.

These contests of speed were also very unsafe and illegal because of the high speeds. So police officers began to attend the races to make sure they were run safely. Soon the races moved off the streets to military aircraft runways which had been constructed across the United States during World War II.

At this time, the standard distance of a drag race was established. A quarter-mile was chosen because it allowed the drivers to reach high speeds, with enough runway space left to slow the cars down safely.

In 1951, the National Hot Rod Association (NHRA) was formed by Wally Parks. Parks was the editor of Hot Rod, an automobile

racing magazine. NHRA is called a sanctioning body, which means the organization sets the rules for racing, including how the cars are built.

NHRA also decides the prize money for the winners and sets up a point system that determines which driver is the national champion at the end of the racing season. Drivers receive a certain number of points at each race, depending on how fast they finish. The driver with the most points at the end of the racing season is named national champion. The first official NHRA national event was held in 1955. About 300 drivers entered this very first race.

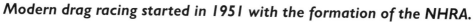

Modern drag racing started in 1951 with the formation of the NHRA.

–Drag Racing Classes

Although there are around 170 different types or classes of drag racing, there are three professional classes of drag racing cars, which are called dragsters. They are: Top Fuel, Funny Car, and Pro Stock. All dragsters at a drag race have lettering painted on them to show the class they belong to. Top Fuel dragsters are lettered TF; Funny Cars are lettered FC; and Pro Stock cars are lettered PRO.

Top Fuel dragsters are the fastest-accelerating cars in the world and the quickest cars at the track. They have long, thin bodies and high wings over the rear tires. They produce a lot of noise at the track. Wearing ear plugs is important when watching these cars race. Top Fuel cars burn nitromethane fuel, which helps the engines produce 4,000 horsepower. These cars are fast!

Funny Cars also use nitromethane for fuel. These cars have fiberglass bodies which are usually left open at the front when the car isn't racing. The fiberglass body must look like a current automobile that you see on the streets.

The Pro Stock car has an air scoop on the hood of the car. These cars also have actual doors and other features you see on regular automobiles. Pro Stock cars use gasoline instead of nitromethane for fuel.

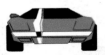

–The Strip

The track that drag racers race on is called a drag strip. The strip is flat and straight. It is an asphalt surface about 4,000 feet long (1,219 meters) with two lanes each 30 feet (9 meters) wide.

A stripe runs down the middle of the track to separate the two lanes. A driver is never allowed to go into the lane of the other driver. Concrete walls or steel guardrails run along the sides of the track past the finish line. The walls help protect a driver by keeping the car on the track if there is an accident.

Sometimes concrete is used on the track from the starting line through the first 50 (15 m) to 400 feet (122 m) of the track. This is called the launching pad. The concrete provides a smooth surface and better traction for the cars when they start to accelerate.

The strip is 4000 feet (1,219 m) long and 60 (18 m) feet wide.

The distance of the drag race is 1,320 feet (402 meters). This leaves 2,680 feet (817 meters) of the track left. What is this section used for? When a dragster travels fast, sometimes over 300 mph (483 kph), it needs enough space to slow down. This is called the "shutdown area" of the track.

The length of the shutdown area can differ from track to track. Drivers should find out the length of the shutdown area before they race, so they will know how much room they have to slow down! Once a driver crosses the finish line on the drag strip, the driver must exit onto one of the many turnoff roads near the shutdown area to get out of the way for other racers.

-Christmas Tree Lights

When drag racing first began, the races were started by a flag person. The winner was decided by a second person who stood at the finish line. As the cars went faster and finished closer together, it became harder to determine the winner of the race. So the "Christmas tree" was developed to start a drag race. It is called a Christmas tree because of the colorful lights which look like those on an actual evergreen Christmas tree.

When the pre-stage and stage lights are lit for both drivers, the start button is pressed, lighting up the rest of the Christmas tree. The rest of the tree has three amber lights, a green light, and a red light down each side of the tree.

The three amber lights flash from top to bottom after the starter pushes the start button. The green light signals the start of the race. The red light means the driver took off before the start signal.

Opposite page: A dragster at the 1991 NHRA Winter Nationals in Pomona, CA.

−From the Cockpit

The interior of a dragster (called a cockpit) doesn't look anything like a regular car. Most of the changes are made for the safety and protection of the driver. The inside of every car at a drag strip looks different. Parts are placed in different areas based on both the driving style and the physical size of the driver.

The driver should have the car set up so that everything is comfortable and all buttons are easy to reach. Gauges, which show the gas, oil, and water levels, should be placed in a spot where the driver can easily see them.

The gear shifter is located either to the right of the driver or most commonly between the driver's legs. Drag racing gear shifts are stronger than in regular cars. Usually, a couple buttons need to be pressed to shift the gears.

The driver's area must have a fire extinguishing system. A fire extinguisher lever is often mounted on the hand brake. If there is a fire, the driver can flip the switch and the extinguisher will go off.

Electrical switches are placed above the driver's head or on the dashboard. These switches will turn off the fuel pump, ignition, water pump, and electric fan. If there is a fire, the driver needs to

be able to reach the fuel shutoff switch quickly and turn it off, so no more fuel is released into the engine.

Five seat belts, called safety harnesses, make sure the driver won't be moved out of place. Some types of dragsters even have arm harnesses to keep the arms from going outside of the cars.

A sturdy chassis or roll cage is required on all dragsters. The chassis looks like the skeleton of a car. The chassis consists of chrome-moly tubing, which was first used on aircraft. The tubing is heated and easy to bend to form a frame for the car. All pieces must fit perfectly in order for the chassis to work. The chassis must be very strong to protect the driver if there is a crash.

A driver preparing his dragster. Notice the steering wheel is still not connected.

–Starting With a Spark

A Top Fuel dragster does not have some parts that are found on other types of race cars. There is no self-starter, suspension, battery, radio, or many other electronics. All the dragster needs is a long, hot spark.

There is electric current running through the car, otherwise there would be no spark. That electrical current comes from a part called a magneto. Magnetos make a spark that lasts a long time. Magnetos produce about 6.5 AC (alternating current) amps. A magneto will last eight to nine minutes. But since the engine life of a Top Fuel dragster is less than two minutes, the magnetos will never run very long.

After each race, the engine is taken completely apart and must be rebuilt with new parts. The pit crew begins to tear the engine down as soon as it is towed back to the pit area. Some pit crews are able to take an engine apart and put it back together in just seven minutes!

Both Top Fuel dragsters and Funny Cars use nitromethane fuel instead of gasoline. Nitromethane is an oily, colorless liquid which has also been used to propel a rocket into space. So you can imagine the explosive charge nitromethane gives to a dragster to help it speed down the drag strip! Nitromethane has a vapor like hot chili peppers. It can cause your eyes to water and your nose

to run. It is used as a fuel for dragsters, rockets, and model airplanes. The liquid is also used as part of the recipe for some medicines and cleaning solutions. For dragsters, a great deal of oil is mixed with the nitromethane before adding it to the car. Racers must be very careful when working with or mixing nitromethane. It is a powerful chemical that could cause a big explosion.

A dragster must be taken apart and rebuilt after each race.

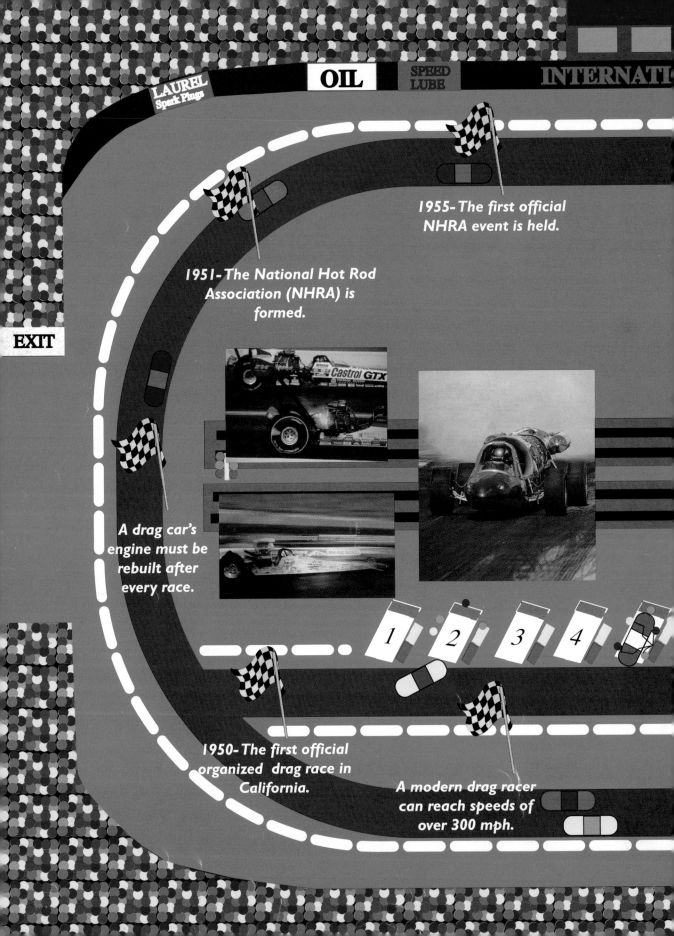

LAUREL
Spark Plugs

OIL

SPEED LUBE

INTERNATI

EXIT

1955- The first official NHRA event is held.

1951- The National Hot Rod Association (NHRA) is formed.

Castrol GTX

A drag car's engine must be rebuilt after every race.

1   2   3   4

1950- The first official organized drag race in California.

A modern drag racer can reach speeds of over 300 mph.

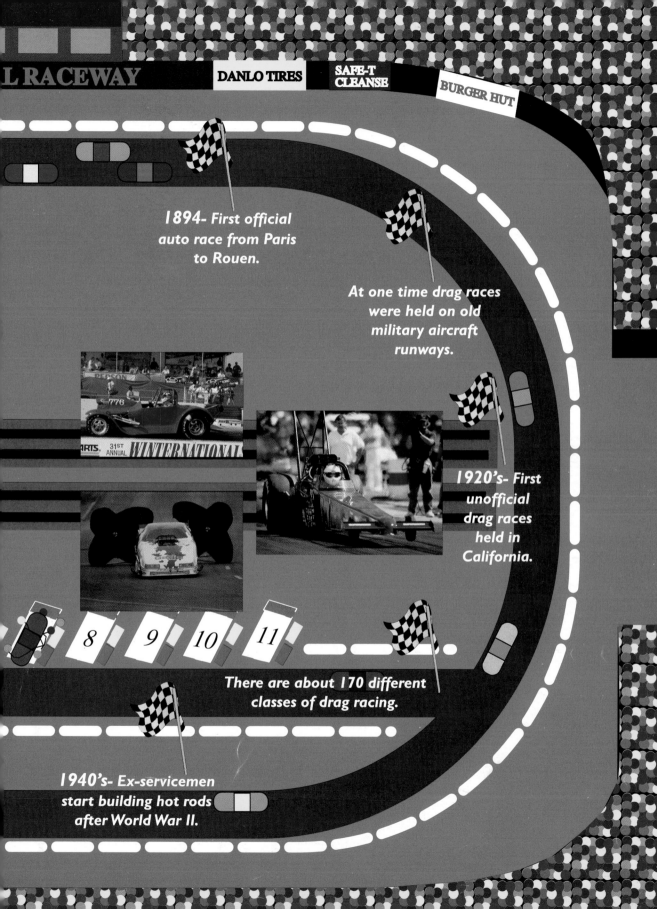

L RACEWAY   DANLO TIRES   SAFE-T CLEANSE   BURGER HUT

1894- First official auto race from Paris to Rouen.

At one time drag races were held on old military aircraft runways.

1920's- First unofficial drag races held in California.

8 9 10 11

There are about 170 different classes of drag racing.

1940's- Ex-servicemen start building hot rods after World War II.

–Driver Gear

Every bit of clothing the driver wears must be made of special safety materials. Drag racers must wear driving suits that are fireproof and usually made of a material called Polybenzimidazole or PBI. PBI does not melt or burn. Socks, gloves, shoes, even underwear must also be fireproof. This is to protect the driver in the case of an engine fire while driving or during a crash.

A high-quality helmet is one of the most important pieces of the driver's gear. The helmet could save a driver's life during a crash. A sharp blow to the helmet, or even scratches and dents can weaken the helmet. Most drivers go through several helmets in a season.

Dragsters use tires that are called drag slicks. The performance of the drag slicks depends on how hot or cool the track is. The temperature of the track will affect the traction of the tires. Traction is how well the tires grip to the track.

Drag slicks will grip the best on a smooth, dry surface. On a hot day, the oils from the asphalt track make the track greasy and slick. The same is true with the tread (or grooves) of rubber tires.

Opposite page: A helmet is one of the most important pieces of equipment for a driver.

When hot, the oils from the tread of the tires come to the surface. In cold weather the tread of the tires becomes harder. Therefore, the tires won't grip to the track surface. In order for the tires to perform properly, they must be heated. This is done by performing a burnout.

-The Burnout

A dragster spins its back wheels just before the start of a race. This is called doing a burnout. Burnouts are one of the most fascinating sights at a drag race, with clouds of smoke rising from the tires. Burning out makes the tires hot and sticky so the tires will grip to the track. The tires will not spin when the driver starts to accelerate. This helps make the car run faster.

Burnouts leave a layer of rubber on the track which the driver drives over while racing. When there are lots of cars racing, the entire quarter-mile track can be lightly coated with rubber. After several burnouts, too much rubber can build up on the track. If the rubber on the track starts to crack and peel, it will be removed with blowtorches and scrapers.

When racers first started doing burnouts before the race, they poured a little liquid bleach in front of the tires. This was supposed to make the tires clean. Now the only type of liquid allowed on the track for a burnout is water.

Burnouts make the tires sticky just before the start of the race.

−Braking and Entering

Once the racer starts to get close to the finish line, it's time to think about braking. The race is over at the finish line. There is no reason to continue going fast. If a driver keeps speeding, the engine could be damaged or the driver could drive off the end of the track if the shutdown area is too small.

Braking fast as the driver crosses the finish line and enters the shutdown area is not good to do either. The racer could lose control of the car, and the tires could smoke and squeal. It is best to lift the foot off the gas pedal just before crossing the finish line. Braking when a car is going over 100 mph (160 kph) must be done carefully. Stopping a car is just as important as starting it!

When a driver crosses the finish line of the drag strip, the driver may use a parachute to slow down the car. The racing parachute is considered to be one of the most important safety items on a dragster. The parachute has saved many racers' lives when the cars have gone out of control or have failed to stop.

A drag racing parachute is five or six times thicker than a regular jumper's parachute. Most cars that go over 150 mph (241 kph) use parachutes. This includes the Top Fuel cars, which are the fastest of the dragsters. Top Fuel cars usually use two parachutes. Parachutes can help lower the speed of the car much

smoother than braking. The driver should always place a hand on the parachute lever much earlier before reaching the finish line. This way, if something goes wrong during the race, the parachute is ready to be pulled. After pulling the parachute lever and opening the parachute, the parachute will need to be picked up. Dragging the parachute can cause damage to it. The team car waits at the end of the drag strip to tow the dragster and parachute back to the trailer.

A dragster uses two parachutes that are six times thicker than a normal parachute.

–Time Trials

Thursday is usually the first day of race week. This is the day the racers try to figure out the setup of the car for the next three days. If teams plan to experiment with any new equipment, they usually try it on the first time trial run on Thursday. A time trial run is a practice run that will determine if the driver races in the race on Sunday. There are only 16 cars allowed in the race. There are five time trial runs during the first three days of race week. There is only one time trial run on Thursday.

During the three practice days, the driver and crew chief work closely together to get the best time trial numbers before the race on Sunday. The crew chief is in charge of the pit crew and helping to prepare the car. The crew chief also works with the engine builder to make sure the engine is running fine.

The pit crew is made up of team members who change the tires and make sure all the parts of the car are working. Crew members also mix the fuel and add it to the car before the race. Before the race, the pit crew rolls the car out onto the drag strip so it is ready for the race.

On Friday, there are two time trial runs. Those drivers who didn't do so well on Thursday have another chance to try to hit a fast speed. On Friday afternoon, there is usually a Top Qualifier

for the weekend. A Top Qualifier is the driver who has the fastest time of the weekend.

Saturday is very important to a driver. It is the last chance the driver will have to qualify for the race. It is also the last chance the pit crew will have to set up the car before the race. This includes working on the engine, brakes, and handling of the car.

By Saturday, the track may have a lot of rubber from the tires on it from the last two days of trials. This makes the starts a little harder. Those who already qualified on Friday still make trial runs, but they don't have to worry about a spot in the race. These drivers now just try to improve their speeds. There are two time trial runs on Saturday.

Bud King at the 1996 NHRA Winter Nationals.

–Passing Inspection

Before a driver is allowed to race, the car must go through a technical inspection by race officials. An inspector looks for anything that might be wrong with the car. The inspector looks for items like safety harnesses and leaking oil.

One of the inspections is weighing the car with electric scales. Every driver, with all gear on, must be weighed with the car to make sure it meets the weight requirements for the class of drag racing.

The funny car is another form of dragster.

Officials also open the hood of the car and check the engine and the other parts inside. Besides being inspected before the race, all competing cars can be inspected during or after the race as well. If the car is in good condition, the car will pass inspection.

Doug Rose in his jet dragster the "Green Momba."
Jet dragsters use airplane jet engines.

-Race Day

On Sunday, the practice is over. This is the big race day. A drag race is not like other types of races, which have about 35 racers racing at the same time. In drag racing, there are 16 cars competing, two at a time. This means there are eight rounds. Two cars race down the strip. The loser is out of the competition. The winner moves on. When all eight rounds are done, there are eight racers left.

The races will now be more evenly matched. The drivers who are competing against each other have already won their race in the first round. After round two, there are only four racers left. The pit crews work frantically, trying to fix anything that broke during the first two rounds. Two of the cars race, followed by the other two cars. Now there are only two cars left for the final round.

The final two drivers roll up to the Christmas tree. There are no more chances. This is it. The light flashes green, and the cars are off. These two drivers give everything they have to cross the finish line first. One is the champion, the other is runner-up. The teams celebrate, pack up, and head for the next track. On Thursday, the drivers and teams start all over again.

Top: *Joe Amato at the 1989 Summer nationals.*
Bottom: *Two dragsters battle it out at the starting line.*

– Junior Drag Racing League

If you would like to know what it's like to drive a car such as a Top Fuel dragster, the NHRA has made this possible. If you are between 8 and 16 years old, you can join the Junior Drag Racing League. The league holds events all over the country. An estimated 5,000 kids participate in Jr. Drag Racing.

Many times a local track will provide Jr. Dragsters for racing. Some racers save their money and buy their own cars to compete in races around their local area. Most Jr. Dragsters cost about $3,000 fully-equipped.

Jr. Dragster drivers compete over a 1/8-mile (1.2 km) distance, reaching speeds of 40 mph (64 kph). The track has plenty of room for a safe shutdown area once the two drivers cross the finish line. The races are usually held on stadium parking lots and other paved areas. Jr. Dragsters have a five horsepower Briggs and Stratton engine. For more information on racing, check with your local drag strip.

A dragster can produce 4000 horsepower and go over 300 miles per hour (483 kph).

–Glossary

Asphalt - The surface of the drag strip.

Chassis/roll cage - The frame of the car. The chassis is like a skeleton of the car.

Christmas tree - An electronic starting system made up of a series of lights. The lights are yellow, amber, green, and red.

Cockpit - The interior of the dragster where the driver sits.

Crew Chief - The crew chief is in charge of organizing the pit crew, overseeing the preparation of the car, and working with the engine builder.

Drag Slicks - The type of tires used on dragsters.

Drag Strip - The 4000 feet (1,219 meters) of straight track which drag racers race on.

Dragsters - Drag racing cars.

Fuel Shutoff Switch - A switch located above the driver's head or on the dashboard which shuts off the fuel. This is an important switch if there is a fire.

Funny Cars - Dragsters with a fiberglass body which is a replica of a current automobile that you see on the streets.

Junior Drag Racing League - A drag racing organization for children ages 8 to 16.

Launching Pad - Concrete used on the track from the starting line through the first 50 (15m) to 400 feet (122 meters) of the track.

Magneto - Electric current that produces a long, hot spark.

National Hot Rod Association - (NHRA) The sanctioning organization for drag racing which sets the rules for racing, including how the cars are built.

Nitromethane - The fuel used in Funny Cars and Top Fuel Dragsters.

Parachute - Drag racing parachute used to slow down cars going 150 mph (241 kph) and faster. Racing parachutes are much thicker than a jumper's parachute.

PBI - Polybenzimidazole, a fireproof material used in driver's suits, gloves, socks, and underwear.

Pit Crew - Members of the race team who help change tires and refuel during the race.

Pre-stage Lights - The top lights on the Christmas tree. The pre-stage lights will light up when your front tires are seven inches from the starting line.

Pro Stock - Dragsters with an air scoop on the hood of the car. These cars also have actual doors and other features you see on regular automobiles. Pro Stock use gasoline.

Stage Lights - The second set of the Christmas tree lights on the Christmas tree. These lights go on as you get closer to the start line.

Time Trial - A time trial run is a practice run that will determine if the driver qualifies to race on Sunday. There are five time trials before the race.

Top Fuel - The fastest accelerating cars in the world. They have long, thin bodies, and high wings over the rear tires.

Top Qualifier - The driver who has the fastest time of the weekend.

—*Internet Sites*

Formula 1 Links Heaven
http://ireland.iol.ie/~roym/
This site includes official sites, latest news, drivers, teams, computer games, circuits, mailing lists. This site has sound and video, very colorful and interactive.

Drag Racing on the net
http://www.lm.com/~hemi/
This is a cool and interactive sight with sound and fun photos.

Indyphoto.com
http://www.indyphoto.com/index.htm
This award winning site has excellent photographs of Indy Cars and it is updated on a regular basis.

MotorSports Image Online
http://www.msimage.com/index2.htm
This site gives you standings, results, schedules, teams, news, and a photo gallery.

Extreme Off-Road Racing
http://www.calpoly.edu/~jcallan/
This site has pre-runners, chat rooms, videos, racing pictures, wrecks, links, and much more extreme off-road racing stuff.

These sites are subject to change. Go to your favorite search engine and type in car racing for more sites.

Pass It On

Racing Enthusiasts: educate readers around the country by passing on information you've learned about car racing. Share your little-known facts and interesting stories. Tell others what your favorite kind of car is or who your favorite racer is. We want to hear from you!

To get posted on the ABDO & Daughters website E-mail us at "Sports@abdopub.com"

Visit the ABDO & Daughter website at www.abdopub.com

–Index